Tahauya Jackson, MBA is the Foun~ ᵈ
Pieces and ~~ ~
of fai
from t
thems~ ~~~er, Tahauya
is devo~ ~~~~ng her story with the world so that
women and girls can find truth in theirs. Her
purpose is to awaken the fight within women
worldwide by equipping them with the strategies,
tools and love to take their power back and thrive in
every area of their lives. As a Certified Life Coach,
Trauma Professional and the epitome of the word
'conqueror,' she shows women daily how to
overcome the same experiences and emotional
trauma that once held her back in life by negatively
affecting her mind, body, soul and spirit.

The Purpose of this Journal

This journal was designed to help women navigate their healing journey, discover their true self and learn how to manage their emotions – all while growing a closer relationship with God.

Printed in the United States of America
First Printing, 2010

www.tahauyajackson.com
Design & Layout by Pam Cayago of Clever Clover Creatives

Real growth is when you start checking and correcting yourself.

Instead of blaming others, you take your power back by being responsible for your life.

Hey Girl,

Heal

SELF-DEVELOPMENT JOURNAL

BY *Tahauya Jackson*, MBA

You can't
HEAL
what you don't
REVEAL.

How to Use this Journal

Today, I feel ...

When we hear the question, "How are you?" our instinctive response is, "I'm fine" — despite the fact that we may not be fine at all. Society has forced us to wear a mask when it comes to how we're feeling by bearing the weight of the world on our shoulders, feeling weak and forcing a smile. Use this section of the journal to be open and honest about how you're really feeling on each specific day and work to get better daily.

Mornings with the Master

How you start your mornings, sets the tone for your day. What better way to start your mornings than with the Master. This prayer section allows you to be strategic with your prayers by following the **PRAY** acronym to structure your talks with God.
Praise. **R**epentance. **A**sking. **Yes** - *this is where you pray God's promises over your life.*

Today's Declaration

Declarations allow you to be intentional about what is coming your way by stating what you want and when you want it. Be intentional about what is coming your way by stating what you want and when you want it. Life and death lie in the power of your tongue, so begin to declare the exact things that you want to manifest in your life. Commit to a specific result and/or experience and declare it to the world and yourself daily. (*I declare this is how it will go, this is what I will create, and what I will have in my life.*)

My "ME" Time

Commit to doing one thing every day that makes you happy! This looks like uninterrupted time free from distractions or anyone else -- just to focus on you. Be intentional about making and spending time for yourself, this will increase your happiness, productivity and better your mental health.

Goals & Expectations

God tells us to "Write the vision and make it plain," because where there is no vision, the people will perish. This is not the season to "go with the flow," you need a solid plan to fulfill the purpose of your life. Every day that we wake up is a blessing to experience new opportunities, so be sure to set a goal for yourself and start your day always expecting the best.

How to Use this Journal

Inner Battery %

Life is full of people, circumstances and priorities that are capable of draining our energy. It's important that we don't attempt to pour from an empty cup. Make it a priority to take time to refuel and rejuvenate your inner self daily to ensure that you are operating at your best and maximizing your potential.

Today's struggles

What issues did you face today? Who pissed you off? What areas were you triggered in? What made you cry? Take some time to reflect in this section on the things that went wrong or bothered you on each particular day that you journal.

Face Your Feelings

I felt like this today because... what led you to experiencing the feelings that you had today? This section can be used for both positive and negative feelings to keep track of your emotional patterns.

Shift Your Mind

Think about how you could do things differently going forward that will be more beneficial to your mental health -- allowing your good days to significantly outweigh your bad days. Reframe your thoughts, manage your emotions and change your perspective in order to grow and live an abundant life.

Speak to it

Scripture can be used as medicine to treat however you're feeling at the time or whatever situation that you're going through. In Isaiah 43:26, God says, "*Put me in remembrance,*" which means to remind God of His word and His promises. Take authority, open your mouth and pray God's word back to Him - it will not return void. Pray with everything that you have believing that what you prayed for, you will receive. Use scriptures to speak to your issues and ask God to change your circumstances.

How to Use this Journal

Mental Health Check

Your mental health is important and so are you! Take some time to reflect on how you're doing mentally on a daily basis. Answer based on a scale of 1-10, with 1 being "I am in a dark place and need help" and 10 being "I'm on Cloud 10, I've never felt better."

Describe your day in one word

Focus on using a different word daily to describe your day besides the general mad, happy, sad, etc. Refer to the "Wheel of Emotions" for more information.

Celebrate Yourself - Wins for the Day

What did you do today that required courage? Did you put in work to get you closer to your goals? Did you do anything today to better yourself, your family or your future? Take this quiet time to reflect on the good things that happened to you on each specific day.

Dear God,

"*But since you are like lukewarm water, neither hot nor cold, I will spit you out of my mouth!*" (Revelation 3:16) Make it a priority to be on fire for God by spending time in His presence -- spreading His love and message.

"I forgive me" Letter

You are not to blame for anything that happened to you. You've carried this weight long enough. Stop beating yourself up about it and allowing your past to control your future. Take time to grow from it and let it go. Forgiveness isn't for them - it's for you, but before you forgive anyone...you have to forgive yourself. It's time to break free!

The "Old Me" Prevention Plan

As we grow in life, we are tempted by the negative circumstances that we've overcome, which try to drag us back to our past. All of our "Old Me's" or alter egos are at different stages of life, but it is crucial to put a plan into place to be sure you don't navigate down the path that you've fought so hard to break free from or pick back up the negative behaviors and/or habits that you once had. *Create a plan of action for things that you could do prior to returning back to your old ways or self - if triggered.*

Mood Tracker

PINK

joyful, happy
relaxed, silly,
content, great

BLUE

sad, lonely,
depressed,
insecure, numb

GREEN

productive,
motivated,
energetic,
active, alive

YELLOW

sick, tired,
unmotivated,
bored, dull,
lazy

ORANGE

average,
normal,
uneventful,
good

RED

angry,
anxious,
frustrated,
annoyed

	JAN	FEB	MAR	APR	MAY	JUN	JUL	AUG	SEP	OCT	NOV	DEC
1												
2												
3												
4												
5												
6												
7												
8												
9												
10												
11												
12												
13												
14												
15												
16												
17												
18												
19												
20												
21												
22												
23												
24												
25												
26												
27												
28												
29												
30												
31												

Self Reflection

I need to heal from

....

....

I need to forgive

....

....

I need to cut off

....

....

I need to let go of

....

....

I need help with

....

....

I need to overcome

....

....

Self Reflection

I need to love

....

....

I need to learn

....

....

I need to improve in

....

....

I need to save

....

....

I need to change

....

....

I'm proud of myself for

....

....

The woman you're becoming will cost you people, relationships, spaces and materials things.

Choose her over everything.

I am Committed to My Healing Because

The things that you don't heal from will spill over into your career, business, children, relationships, finances and every area of your life. What areas of your life will become better as you heal?

My triggers are...

Until we work on healing our triggers, we will continue to react to the same problems and situations the same way.

Embrace your Experiences

During the course of my life, I have experienced:

Pain to Power

My experiences have taught me:

As a result, I've grown:

Honesty Hour

These people/things hurt me:

....

....

Negative behaviors that I now have:

....

....

I need to apologize to:

....

....

I make excuses for:

....

....

My void fillers:

....

....

I'm addicted to:

....

....

Honesty Hour

Things holding me back:

....

....

Bad habits that I need to break:

....

....

Generational curses that have affected my life:

....

....

Things that I *love* about myself

Things that I am grateful for

♡ ....

♡ ....

♡ ....

♡

♡ ....

♡ ....

♡ ....

♡

♡ ....

♡ ....

♡ ....

♡

"I forgive me" Letter

Dear _____,

I forgive you for ....

....

....

....

....

....

....

....

....

....

....

....

....

....

....

....

The "Old Me" Prevention Plan

Get serious -- about your healing.

Get serious -- about your peace.

Get serious -- about your future.

Get serious -- about your goals.

Get serious -- about your love.

Get serious -- about your faith.

Get serious -- about your mental.

Get serious -- about your life.

Get serious -- about yourself.

Long story short ...

you got this!

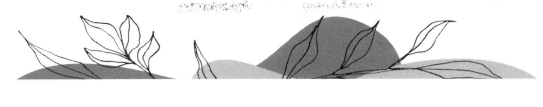

Dream Life Chart

When you change your thoughts, you change your life and only
YOU have the power to change your circumstances.

What do you want in each area? Be specific. Write out what this looks like for you.

FAMILY

FINANCES

BUSINESS / CAREER

SPIRITUALITY

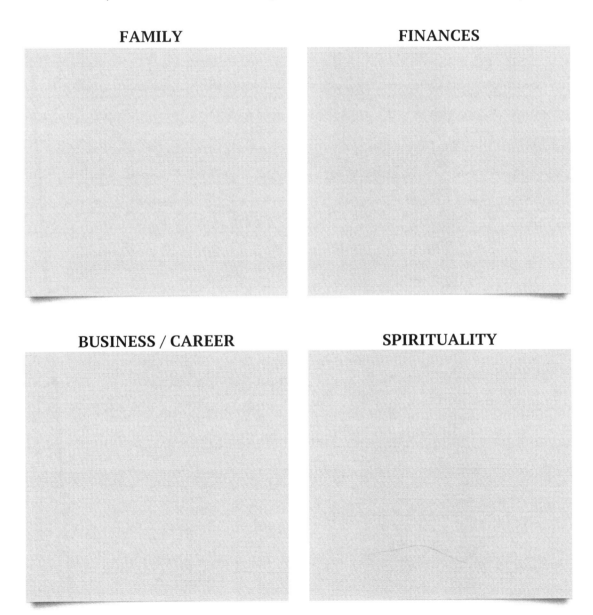

Quarterly Goals

+ ACTION PLAN

Quarter 1 2 3 4

<u>Goals</u>

<u>Steps</u>

Quarter 1 2 3 4

<u>Goals</u>

<u>Steps</u>

I am believing in God for...

MONTH _____

1

2

3

4

MONTH _____

1

2

3

4

MONTH _____

1

2

3

4

The ugly part of your story you're living through right now is going to be one of the most powerful parts of your testimony.

It may have broken your heart, but it opened your eyes.

Take that win.

Rise & Shine

"
God has never birthed a failure, now go be GREAT today.

Inner battery _____ %

Today, I feel:

Mornings with the Master

Lord, I thank you for:

Please forgive me for:

Father, please bless:

Lord, you promised me:

I need to talk to you about:

Today's declaration:

Make time for ME:

Goals & Expectations:

Reflect & Release

Just when the caterpillar thought her life was over, she began to fly.

Date _____

Inner battery _____ %

Celebrate yourself - Wins for the day:

Today's struggles:

Face your feelings:

Shift your mind:

Speak to it:

MENTAL HEALTH CHECK | On a scale of 1-10, how are you feeling?

1	2	3	4	5	6	7	8	9	10

Describe your day in 1 word:

Dear God,

Rise & Shine

66
God has never birthed a failure, now go be GREAT today.

Date _____

Inner battery _____ %

Today, I feel:

Mornings with the Master

Lord, I thank you for:

Please forgive me for:

Father, please bless:

Lord, you promised me:

I need to talk to you about:

Today's declaration:

Make time for ME:

Goals & Expectations:

Reflect & Release

> Just when the caterpillar thought her life was over, she began to fly.

Date _____

Inner battery _____ %

Celebrate yourself - Wins for the day:

Today's struggles:

Face your feelings:

Shift your mind:

Speak to it:

MENTAL HEALTH CHECK | On a scale of 1-10, how are you feeling?

| 1 | 2 | 3 | 4 | 5 | 6 | 7 | 8 | 9 | 10 |

Describe your day in 1 word:

Dear God,

Rise & Shine

> *God has never birthed a failure, now go be GREAT today.*

Today, I feel:

Mornings with the Master

Lord, I thank you for:

Please forgive me for:

Father, please bless:

Lord, you promised me:

I need to talk to you about:

Today's declaration:

Make time for ME:

Goals & Expectations:

Reflect & Release

" Just when the caterpillar thought her life was over, she began to fly.

Date _____

Inner battery _____ %

Celebrate yourself - Wins for the day:

Today's struggles:

Face your feelings:

Shift your mind:

Speak to it:

MENTAL HEALTH CHECK | On a scale of 1-10, how are you feeling?

| 1 | 2 | 3 | 4 | 5 | 6 | 7 | 8 | 9 | 10 |

Describe your day in 1 word:

Dear God,

Rise & Shine

"

God has never birthed a failure, now go be GREAT today.

Date _____

Inner battery _____ %

Today, I feel:

Mornings with the Master

Lord, I thank you for:

Please forgive me for:

Father, please bless:

Lord, you promised me:

I need to talk to you about:

Today's declaration:

Make time for ME:

Goals & Expectations:

Reflect & Release

Just when the caterpillar thought her life was over, she began to fly.

Date _____

Inner battery _____ %

Celebrate yourself - Wins for the day:

Today's struggles:

Face your feelings:

Shift your mind:

Speak to it:

MENTAL HEALTH CHECK | On a scale of 1-10, how are you feeling?

1	2	3	4	5	6	7	8	9	10

Describe your day in 1 word:

Dear God,

Rise & Shine

"
God has never birthed a failure, now go be GREAT today.

Date _____

Inner battery _____ %

Today, I feel:

Mornings with the Master

Lord, I thank you for:

Please forgive me for:

Father, please bless:

Lord, you promised me:

I need to talk to you about:

Today's declaration:

Make time for ME:

Goals & Expectations:

Reflect & Release

Date _____

Inner battery _____ %

> Just when the caterpillar thought her life was over, she
> began to fly.

Celebrate yourself - Wins for the day:

Today's struggles:

Face your feelings:

Shift your mind:

Speak to it:

MENTAL HEALTH CHECK | On a scale of 1-10, how are you feeling?

1	2	3	4	5	6	7	8	9	10

Describe your day in 1 word:

Dear God,

Rise & Shine

" God has never birthed a failure, now go be GREAT today.

Today, I feel:

Mornings with the Master

Lord, I thank you for:

Please forgive me for:

Father, please bless:

Lord, you promised me:

I need to talk to you about:

Today's declaration:

Make time for ME:

Goals & Expectations:

Reflect & Release

Just when the caterpillar thought her life was over, she began to fly.

Date _____

Inner battery _____ %

Celebrate yourself - Wins for the day:

Today's struggles:

Face your feelings:

Shift your mind:

Speak to it:

MENTAL HEALTH CHECK | On a scale of 1-10, how are you feeling?

1	2	3	4	5	6	7	8	9	10

Describe your day in 1 word:

Dear God,

Rise & Shine

Date _____

Inner battery _____ %

Today, I feel:

Mornings with the Master

Lord, I thank you for:

Please forgive me for:

Father, please bless:

Lord, you promised me:

I need to talk to you about:

Today's declaration:

Make time for ME:

Goals & Expectations:

Reflect & Release

66

Just when the caterpillar thought her life was over, she began to fly.

Date _____

Inner battery _____ %

Celebrate yourself - Wins for the day:

Today's struggles:

Face your feelings:

Shift your mind:

Speak to it:

MENTAL HEALTH CHECK | On a scale of 1-10, how are you feeling?

| 1 | 2 | 3 | 4 | 5 | 6 | 7 | 8 | 9 | 10 |

Describe your day in 1 word:

Dear God,

Rise & Shine

God has never birthed a failure, now go be GREAT today.

Today, I feel:

Mornings with the Master

Lord, I thank you for:

Please forgive me for:

Father, please bless:

Lord, you promised me:

I need to talk to you about:

Today's declaration:

Make time for ME:

Goals & Expectations:

Reflect & Release

Just when the caterpillar thought her life was over, she began to fly.

Date _____

Inner battery _____ %

Celebrate yourself - Wins for the day:

Today's struggles:

Face your feelings:

Shift your mind:

Speak to it:

MENTAL HEALTH CHECK | On a scale of 1-10, how are you feeling?

1	2	3	4	5	6	7	8	9	10

Describe your day in 1 word:

Dear God,

Rise & Shine

" *God has never birthed a failure, now go be GREAT today.*

Today, I feel:

Mornings with the Master

Lord, I thank you for:

Please forgive me for:

Father, please bless:

Lord, you promised me:

I need to talk to you about:

Today's declaration:

Make time for ME:

Goals & Expectations:

Reflect & Release

" Just when the caterpillar thought her life was over, she began to fly.

Date _____

Inner battery _____ %

Celebrate yourself - Wins for the day:

Today's struggles:

Face your feelings:

Shift your mind:

Speak to it:

MENTAL HEALTH CHECK | On a scale of 1-10, how are you feeling?

| 1 | 2 | 3 | 4 | 5 | 6 | 7 | 8 | 9 | 10 |

Describe your day in 1 word:

Dear God,

Rise & Shine

66

God has never birthed a failure, now go be GREAT today.

Date _____

Inner battery _____ %

Today, I feel:

Mornings with the Master

Lord, I thank you for:

Please forgive me for:

Father, please bless:

Lord, you promised me:

I need to talk to you about:

Today's declaration:

Make time for ME:

Goals & Expectations:

Reflect & Release

"
Just when the caterpillar thought her life was over, she began to fly.

Date _____

Inner battery _____ %

Celebrate yourself - Wins for the day:

Today's struggles:

Face your feelings:

Shift your mind:

Speak to it:

MENTAL HEALTH CHECK | On a scale of 1-10, how are you feeling?

1	2	3	4	5	6	7	8	9	10

Describe your day in 1 word:

Dear God,

Rise & Shine

Date _____

> *God has never birthed a failure, now go be GREAT today.*

Inner battery _____ %

Today, I feel:

Mornings with the Master

Lord, I thank you for:

Please forgive me for:

Father, please bless:

Lord, you promised me:

I need to talk to you about:

Today's declaration:

Make time for ME:

Goals & Expectations:

Reflect & Release

> "
Just when the caterpillar thought her life was over, she began to fly.

Date _____

Inner battery _____ %

Celebrate yourself - Wins for the day:

Today's struggles:

Face your feelings:

Shift your mind:

Speak to it:

MENTAL HEALTH CHECK | On a scale of 1-10, how are you feeling?

| 1 | 2 | 3 | 4 | 5 | 6 | 7 | 8 | 9 | 10 |

Describe your day in 1 word:

Dear God,

Rise & Shine

Date _____

Inner battery _____ %

Today, I feel:

Mornings with the Master

Lord, I thank you for:

Please forgive me for:

Father, please bless:

Lord, you promised me:

I need to talk to you about:

Today's declaration:

Make time for ME:

Goals & Expectations:

Reflect & Release

"
Just when the caterpillar thought her life was over, she began to fly.

Date _____

Inner battery _____ %

Celebrate yourself - Wins for the day:

Today's struggles:

Face your feelings:

Shift your mind:

Speak to it:

MENTAL HEALTH CHECK | On a scale of 1-10, how are you feeling?

1	2	3	4	5	6	7	8	9	10

Describe your day in 1 word:

Dear God,

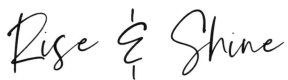

Rise & Shine

> "
> *God has never birthed a failure, now go be GREAT today.*

Today, I feel:

Mornings with the Master

Lord, I thank you for:

Please forgive me for:

Father, please bless:

Lord, you promised me:

I need to talk to you about:

Today's declaration:

Make time for ME:

Goals & Expectations:

Reflect & Release

*Just when the caterpillar thought her life was over, she
began to fly.*

Date _____

Inner battery _____ %

Celebrate yourself - Wins for the day:

Today's struggles:

Face your feelings:

Shift your mind:

Speak to it:

MENTAL HEALTH CHECK | On a scale of 1-10, how are you feeling?

| 1 | 2 | 3 | 4 | 5 | 6 | 7 | 8 | 9 | 10 |

Describe your day in 1 word:

Dear God,

Rise & Shine

" *God has never birthed a failure, now go be GREAT today.*

Today, I feel:

Mornings with the Master

Lord, I thank you for:

Please forgive me for:

Father, please bless:

Lord, you promised me:

I need to talk to you about:

Today's declaration:

Make time for ME:

Goals & Expectations:

Reflect & Release

66
Just when the caterpillar thought her life was over, she began to fly.

Date _____

Inner battery _____ %

Celebrate yourself - Wins for the day:

Today's struggles:

Face your feelings:

Shift your mind:

Speak to it:

MENTAL HEALTH CHECK | On a scale of 1-10, how are you feeling?

| 1 | 2 | 3 | 4 | 5 | 6 | 7 | 8 | 9 | 10 |

Describe your day in 1 word:

Dear God,

Rise & Shine

> God has never birthed a failure, now go be GREAT today.

Date _____

Inner battery _____ %

Today, I feel:

Mornings with the Master

Lord, I thank you for:

Please forgive me for:

Father, please bless:

Lord, you promised me:

I need to talk to you about:

Today's declaration:

Make time for ME:

Goals & Expectations:

Reflect & Release

> ❝
> *Just when the caterpillar thought her life was over, she began to fly.*

Date _____

Inner battery _____ %

Celebrate yourself - Wins for the day:

Today's struggles:

Face your feelings:

Shift your mind:

Speak to it:

MENTAL HEALTH CHECK | On a scale of 1-10, how are you feeling?

1	2	3	4	5	6	7	8	9	10

Describe your day in 1 word:

Dear God,

Rise & Shine

66

God has never birthed a failure, now go be GREAT today.

Inner battery _____ %

Today, I feel:

Mornings with the Master

Lord, I thank you for:

Please forgive me for:

Father, please bless:

Lord, you promised me:

I need to talk to you about:

Today's declaration:

Make time for ME:

Goals & Expectations:

Reflect & Release

66

Just when the caterpillar thought her life was over, she began to fly.

Date _____

Inner battery _____ %

Celebrate yourself - Wins for the day:

Today's struggles:

Face your feelings:

Shift your mind:

Speak to it:

MENTAL HEALTH CHECK | On a scale of 1-10, how are you feeling?

| 1 | 2 | 3 | 4 | 5 | 6 | 7 | 8 | 9 | 10 |

Describe your day in 1 word:

Dear God,

Rise & Shine

> God has never birthed a failure, now go be GREAT today.

Date _____

Inner battery _____ %

Today, I feel:

Mornings with the Master

Lord, I thank you for:

Please forgive me for:

Father, please bless:

Lord, you promised me:

I need to talk to you about:

Today's declaration:

Make time for ME:

Goals & Expectations:

Reflect & Release

66

Just when the caterpillar thought her life was over, she began to fly.

Date _____

Inner battery _____ %

Celebrate yourself - Wins for the day:

Today's struggles:

Face your feelings:

Shift your mind:

Speak to it:

MENTAL HEALTH CHECK | On a scale of 1-10, how are you feeling?

| 1 | 2 | 3 | 4 | 5 | 6 | 7 | 8 | 9 | 10 |

Describe your day in 1 word:

Dear God,

Rise & Shine

Date _____

Inner battery _____ %

Today, I feel:

Mornings with the Master

Lord, I thank you for:

Please forgive me for:

Father, please bless:

Lord, you promised me:

I need to talk to you about:

Today's declaration:

Make time for ME:

Goals & Expectations:

Reflect & Release

" Just when the caterpillar thought her life was over, she
began to fly.

Date _____

Inner battery _____ %

Celebrate yourself - Wins for the day:

Today's struggles:

Face your feelings:

Shift your mind:

Speak to it:

MENTAL HEALTH CHECK | On a scale of 1-10, how are you feeling?

1	2	3	4	5	6	7	8	9	10

Describe your day in 1 word:

Dear God,

Rise & Shine

Date _____

66

God has never birthed a failure, now go be GREAT today.

Inner battery _____ %

Today, I feel:

Mornings with the Master

Lord, I thank you for:

Please forgive me for:

Father, please bless:

Lord, you promised me:

I need to talk to you about:

Today's declaration:

Make time for ME:

Goals & Expectations:

Reflect & Release

"
Just when the caterpillar thought her life was over, she began to fly.

Date _____

Inner battery _____ %

Celebrate yourself - Wins for the day:

Today's struggles:

Face your feelings:

Shift your mind:

Speak to it:

MENTAL HEALTH CHECK | On a scale of 1-10, how are you feeling?

1	2	3	4	5	6	7	8	9	10

Describe your day in 1 word:

Dear God,

Rise & Shine

God has never birthed a failure, now go be GREAT today.

Today, I feel:

Mornings with the Master

Lord, I thank you for:

Please forgive me for:

Father, please bless:

Lord, you promised me:

I need to talk to you about:

Today's declaration:

Make time for ME:

Goals & Expectations:

Reflect & Release

Just when the caterpillar thought her life was over, she began to fly.

Date _____

Inner battery _____ %

Celebrate yourself - Wins for the day:

Today's struggles:

Face your feelings:

Shift your mind:

Speak to it:

MENTAL HEALTH CHECK | On a scale of 1-10, how are you feeling?

1	2	3	4	5	6	7	8	9	10

Describe your day in 1 word:

Dear God,

Rise & Shine

"
God has never birthed a failure, now go be GREAT today.

Date _____

Inner battery _____ %

Today, I feel:

Mornings with the Master

Lord, I thank you for:

Please forgive me for:

Father, please bless:

Lord, you promised me:

I need to talk to you about:

Today's declaration:

Make time for ME:

Goals & Expectations:

Reflect & Release

Just when the caterpillar thought her life was over, she began to fly.

Date _____

Inner battery _____ %

Celebrate yourself - Wins for the day:

Today's struggles:

Face your feelings:

Shift your mind:

Speak to it:

MENTAL HEALTH CHECK | On a scale of 1-10, how are you feeling?

| 1 | 2 | 3 | 4 | 5 | 6 | 7 | 8 | 9 | 10 |

Describe your day in 1 word:

Dear God,

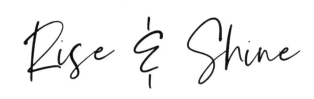

Rise & Shine

"
God has never birthed a failure, now go be GREAT today.

Date _____

Inner battery _____ %

Today, I feel:

Mornings with the Master

Lord, I thank you for:

Please forgive me for:

Father, please bless:

Lord, you promised me:

I need to talk to you about:

Today's declaration:

Make time for ME:

Goals & Expectations:

Reflect & Release

Date _____

Inner battery _____ %

Celebrate yourself - Wins for the day:

Today's struggles:

Face your feelings:

Shift your mind:

Speak to it:

MENTAL HEALTH CHECK | On a scale of 1-10, how are you feeling?

1	2	3	4	5	6	7	8	9	10

Describe your day in 1 word:

Dear God,

Rise & Shine

"
God has never birthed a failure, now go be GREAT today.

Today, I feel:

Mornings with the Master

Lord, I thank you for:

Please forgive me for:

Father, please bless:

Lord, you promised me:

I need to talk to you about:

Today's declaration:

Make time for ME:

Goals & Expectations:

Reflect & Release

"
Just when the caterpillar thought her life was over, she began to fly.

Date _____

Inner battery _____ %

Celebrate yourself - Wins for the day:

Today's struggles:

Face your feelings:

Shift your mind:

Speak to it:

MENTAL HEALTH CHECK | On a scale of 1-10, how are you feeling?

| 1 | 2 | 3 | 4 | 5 | 6 | 7 | 8 | 9 | 10 |

Describe your day in 1 word:

Dear God,

Rise & Shine

God has never birthed a failure, now go be GREAT today.

Inner battery _____ %

Today, I feel:

Mornings with the Master

Lord, I thank you for:

Please forgive me for:

Father, please bless:

Lord, you promised me:

I need to talk to you about:

Today's declaration:

Make time for ME:

Goals & Expectations:

Reflect & Release

"
Just when the caterpillar thought her life was over, she began to fly.

Date _____

Inner battery _____ %

Celebrate yourself - Wins for the day:

Today's struggles:

Face your feelings:

Shift your mind:

Speak to it:

MENTAL HEALTH CHECK | On a scale of 1-10, how are you feeling?

| 1 | 2 | 3 | 4 | 5 | 6 | 7 | 8 | 9 | 10 |

Describe your day in 1 word:

Dear God,

Rise & Shine

Date _____

Inner battery _____ %

Today, I feel:

Mornings with the Master

Lord, I thank you for:

Please forgive me for:

Father, please bless:

Lord, you promised me:

I need to talk to you about:

Today's declaration:

Make time for ME:

Goals & Expectations:

Reflect & Release

Date _____

Inner battery _____ %

Celebrate yourself - Wins for the day:

Today's struggles:

Face your feelings:

Shift your mind:

Speak to it:

MENTAL HEALTH CHECK | On a scale of 1-10, how are you feeling?

1	2	3	4	5	6	7	8	9	10

Describe your day in 1 word:

Dear God,

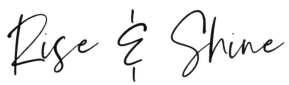

Rise & Shine

> *God has never birthed a failure, now go be GREAT today.*

Today, I feel:

Mornings with the Master

Lord, I thank you for:

Please forgive me for:

Father, please bless:

Lord, you promised me:

I need to talk to you about:

Today's declaration:

Make time for ME:

Goals & Expectations:

Reflect & Release

" Just when the caterpillar thought her life was over, she began to fly.

Date _____

Inner battery _____ %

Celebrate yourself - Wins for the day:

Today's struggles:

Face your feelings:

Shift your mind:

Speak to it:

MENTAL HEALTH CHECK | On a scale of 1-10, how are you feeling?

| 1 | 2 | 3 | 4 | 5 | 6 | 7 | 8 | 9 | 10 |

Describe your day in 1 word:

Dear God,

Rise & Shine

Date _____

Inner battery _____ %

Today, I feel:

Mornings with the Master

Lord, I thank you for:

Please forgive me for:

Father, please bless:

Lord, you promised me:

I need to talk to you about:

Today's declaration:

Make time for ME:

Goals & Expectations:

Reflect & Release

Just when the caterpillar thought her life was over, she began to fly.

Date _____

Inner battery _____ %

Celebrate yourself - Wins for the day:

Today's struggles:

Face your feelings:

Shift your mind:

Speak to it:

MENTAL HEALTH CHECK | On a scale of 1-10, how are you feeling?

| 1 | 2 | 3 | 4 | 5 | 6 | 7 | 8 | 9 | 10 |

Describe your day in 1 word:

Dear God,

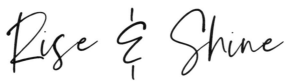

Rise & Shine

Date _____

Inner battery _____ %

Today, I feel:

Mornings with the Master

Lord, I thank you for:

Please forgive me for:

Father, please bless:

Lord, you promised me:

I need to talk to you about:

Today's declaration:

Make time for ME:

Goals & Expectations:

Reflect & Release

" Just when the caterpillar thought her life was over, she began to fly.

Date _____

Inner battery _____ %

Celebrate yourself - Wins for the day:

Today's struggles:

Face your feelings:

Shift your mind:

Speak to it:

MENTAL HEALTH CHECK | On a scale of 1-10, how are you feeling?

| 1 | 2 | 3 | 4 | 5 | 6 | 7 | 8 | 9 | 10 |

Describe your day in 1 word:

Dear God,

Rise & Shine

> "
God has never birthed a failure, now go be GREAT today.

Today, I feel:

Mornings with the Master

Lord, I thank you for:

Please forgive me for:

Father, please bless:

Lord, you promised me:

I need to talk to you about:

Today's declaration:

Make time for ME:

Goals & Expectations:

Reflect & Release

> Just when the caterpillar thought her life was over, she began to fly.

Date _____

Inner battery _____ %

Celebrate yourself - Wins for the day:

Today's struggles:

Face your feelings:

Shift your mind:

Speak to it:

MENTAL HEALTH CHECK | On a scale of 1-10, how are you feeling?

| 1 | 2 | 3 | 4 | 5 | 6 | 7 | 8 | 9 | 10 |

Describe your day in 1 word:

Dear God,

Rise & Shine

Date _____

> *God has never birthed a failure, now go be GREAT today.*

Inner battery _____ %

Today, I feel:

Mornings with the Master

Lord, I thank you for:

Please forgive me for:

Father, please bless:

Lord, you promised me:

I need to talk to you about:

Today's declaration:

Make time for ME:

Goals & Expectations:

Reflect & Release

">>

*Just when the caterpillar thought her life was over, she
began to fly.*

Date _____

Inner battery _____ %

Celebrate yourself - Wins for the day:

Today's struggles:

Face your feelings:

Shift your mind:

Speak to it:

MENTAL HEALTH CHECK | On a scale of 1-10, how are you feeling?

1	2	3	4	5	6	7	8	9	10

Describe your day in 1 word:

Dear God,

Girl, you already have what it takes.

You've got Jesus.

What's broken can
be mended.

What's hurt can be
healed.

No matter how dark
it gets, the sun is
going to rise
again.

Rise & Shine

> God has never birthed a failure, now go be GREAT today.

Today, I feel:

Mornings with the Master

Lord, I thank you for:

Please forgive me for:

Father, please bless:

Lord, you promised me:

I need to talk to you about:

Today's declaration:

Make time for ME:

Goals & Expectations:

Reflect & Release

Just when the caterpillar thought her life was over, she began to fly.

Date _____

Inner battery _____ %

Celebrate yourself - Wins for the day:

Today's struggles:

Face your feelings:

Shift your mind:

Speak to it:

MENTAL HEALTH CHECK | On a scale of 1-10, how are you feeling?

| 1 | 2 | 3 | 4 | 5 | 6 | 7 | 8 | 9 | 10 |

Describe your day in 1 word:

Dear God,

Rise & Shine

"God has never birthed a failure, now go be GREAT today.

Date _____

Inner battery _____ %

Today, I feel:

Mornings with the Master

Lord, I thank you for:

Please forgive me for:

Father, please bless:

Lord, you promised me:

I need to talk to you about:

Today's declaration:

Make time for ME:

Goals & Expectations:

Reflect & Release

66

Just when the caterpillar thought her life was over, she began to fly.

Date _____

Inner battery _____ %

Celebrate yourself - Wins for the day:

Today's struggles:

Face your feelings:

Shift your mind:

Speak to it:

MENTAL HEALTH CHECK | On a scale of 1-10, how are you feeling?

| 1 | 2 | 3 | 4 | 5 | 6 | 7 | 8 | 9 | 10 |

Describe your day in 1 word:

Dear God,

Rise & Shine

> God has never birthed a failure, now go be GREAT today.

Date _____

Inner battery _____ %

Today, I feel:

Mornings with the Master

Lord, I thank you for:

Please forgive me for:

Father, please bless:

Lord, you promised me:

I need to talk to you about:

Today's declaration:

Make time for ME:

Goals & Expectations:

Reflect & Release

Date _____

Inner battery _____ %

" Just when the caterpillar thought her life was over, she began to fly.

Celebrate yourself - Wins for the day:

Today's struggles:

Face your feelings:

Shift your mind:

Speak to it:

MENTAL HEALTH CHECK | On a scale of 1-10, how are you feeling?

1	2	3	4	5	6	7	8	9	10

Describe your day in 1 word:

Dear God,

Rise & Shine

> "
God has never birthed a failure, now go be GREAT today.

Date _____

Inner battery _____ %

Today, I feel:

Mornings with the Master

Lord, I thank you for:

Please forgive me for:

Father, please bless:

Lord, you promised me:

I need to talk to you about:

Today's declaration:

Make time for ME:

Goals & Expectations:

Reflect & Release

Just when the caterpillar thought her life was over, she began to fly.

Date _____

Inner battery _____ %

Celebrate yourself - Wins for the day:

Today's struggles:

Face your feelings:

Shift your mind:

Speak to it:

MENTAL HEALTH CHECK | On a scale of 1-10, how are you feeling?

| 1 | 2 | 3 | 4 | 5 | 6 | 7 | 8 | 9 | 10 |

Describe your day in 1 word:

Dear God,

Rise & Shine

> *God has never birthed a failure, now go be GREAT today.*

Today, I feel:

Mornings with the Master

Lord, I thank you for:

Please forgive me for:

Father, please bless:

Lord, you promised me:

I need to talk to you about:

Today's declaration:

Make time for ME:

Goals & Expectations:

Reflect & Release

"

Just when the caterpillar thought her life was over, she began to fly.

Date _____

Inner battery _____ %

Celebrate yourself - Wins for the day:

Today's struggles:

Face your feelings:

Shift your mind:

Speak to it:

MENTAL HEALTH CHECK | On a scale of 1-10, how are you feeling?

| 1 | 2 | 3 | 4 | 5 | 6 | 7 | 8 | 9 | 10 |

Describe your day in 1 word:

Dear God,

Rise & Shine

Date _____

Inner battery _____ %

God has never birthed a failure, now go be GREAT today.

Today, I feel:

Mornings with the Master

Lord, I thank you for:

Please forgive me for:

Father, please bless:

Lord, you promised me:

I need to talk to you about:

Today's declaration:

Make time for ME:

Goals & Expectations:

Reflect & Release

❝❝

Just when the caterpillar thought her life was over, she began to fly.

Date _____

Inner battery _____ %

Celebrate yourself - Wins for the day:

Today's struggles:

Face your feelings:

Shift your mind:

Speak to it:

MENTAL HEALTH CHECK | On a scale of 1-10, how are you feeling?

| 1 | 2 | 3 | 4 | 5 | 6 | 7 | 8 | 9 | 10 |

Describe your day in 1 word:

Dear God,

Rise & Shine

"
God has never birthed a failure, now go be GREAT today.

Today, I feel:

Mornings with the Master

Lord, I thank you for:

Please forgive me for:

Father, please bless:

Lord, you promised me:

I need to talk to you about:

Today's declaration:

Make time for ME:

Goals & Expectations:

Reflect & Release

Just when the caterpillar thought her life was over, she began to fly.

Date _____

Inner battery _____ %

Celebrate yourself - Wins for the day:

Today's struggles:

Face your feelings:

Shift your mind:

Speak to it:

MENTAL HEALTH CHECK | On a scale of 1-10, how are you feeling?

1	2	3	4	5	6	7	8	9	10

Describe your day in 1 word:

Dear God,

Rise & Shine

> *God has never birthed a failure, now go be GREAT today.*

Date _____

Inner battery _____ %

Today, I feel:

Mornings with the Master

Lord, I thank you for:

Please forgive me for:

Father, please bless:

Lord, you promised me:

I need to talk to you about:

Today's declaration:

Make time for ME:

Goals & Expectations:

Reflect & Release

"
Just when the caterpillar thought her life was over, she began to fly.

Date _____

Inner battery _____ %

Celebrate yourself - Wins for the day:

Today's struggles:

Face your feelings:

Shift your mind:

Speak to it:

MENTAL HEALTH CHECK | On a scale of 1-10, how are you feeling?

| 1 | 2 | 3 | 4 | 5 | 6 | 7 | 8 | 9 | 10 |

Describe your day in 1 word:

Dear God,

Rise & Shine

> ❝
> *God has never birthed a failure, now go be GREAT today.*

Date _____

Inner battery _____ %

Today, I feel:

Mornings with the Master

Lord, I thank you for:

Please forgive me for:

Father, please bless:

Lord, you promised me:

I need to talk to you about:

Today's declaration:

Make time for ME:

Goals & Expectations:

Reflect & Release

Date _____

Inner battery _____ %

Celebrate yourself - Wins for the day:

Today's struggles:

Face your feelings:

Shift your mind:

Speak to it:

MENTAL HEALTH CHECK | On a scale of 1-10, how are you feeling?

| 1 | 2 | 3 | 4 | 5 | 6 | 7 | 8 | 9 | 10 |

Describe your day in 1 word:

Dear God,

Rise & Shine

Date _____

Inner battery _____ %

God has never birthed a failure, now go be GREAT today.

Today, I feel:

Mornings with the Master

Lord, I thank you for:

Please forgive me for:

Father, please bless:

Lord, you promised me:

I need to talk to you about:

Today's declaration:

Make time for ME:

Goals & Expectations:

Reflect & Release

"

Just when the caterpillar thought her life was over, she began to fly.

Date _____

Inner battery _____ %

Celebrate yourself - Wins for the day:

Today's struggles:

Face your feelings:

Shift your mind:

Speak to it:

MENTAL HEALTH CHECK | On a scale of 1-10, how are you feeling?

| 1 | 2 | 3 | 4 | 5 | 6 | 7 | 8 | 9 | 10 |

Describe your day in 1 word:

Dear God,

Rise & Shine

Date _____

Inner battery _____ %

God has never birthed a failure, now go be GREAT today.

Today, I feel:

Mornings with the Master

Lord, I thank you for:

Please forgive me for:

Father, please bless:

Lord, you promised me:

I need to talk to you about:

Today's declaration:

Make time for ME:

Goals & Expectations:

Reflect & Release

> Just when the caterpillar thought her life was over, she began to fly.

Date _____

Inner battery _____ %

Celebrate yourself - Wins for the day:

Today's struggles:

Face your feelings:

Shift your mind:

Speak to it:

MENTAL HEALTH CHECK | On a scale of 1-10, how are you feeling?

| 1 | 2 | 3 | 4 | 5 | 6 | 7 | 8 | 9 | 10 |

Describe your day in 1 word:

Dear God,

Rise & Shine

God has never birthed a failure, now go be GREAT today.

Inner battery _____ %

Today, I feel:

Mornings with the Master

Lord, I thank you for:

Please forgive me for:

Father, please bless:

Lord, you promised me:

I need to talk to you about:

Today's declaration:

Make time for ME:

Goals & Expectations:

Reflect & Release

"

Just when the caterpillar thought her life was over, she began to fly.

Date _____

Inner battery _____ %

Celebrate yourself - Wins for the day:

Today's struggles:

Face your feelings:

Shift your mind:

Speak to it:

MENTAL HEALTH CHECK | On a scale of 1-10, how are you feeling?

| 1 | 2 | 3 | 4 | 5 | 6 | 7 | 8 | 9 | 10 |

Describe your day in 1 word:

Dear God,

Rise & Shine

> God has never birthed a failure, now go be GREAT today.

Date _____

Inner battery _____ %

Today, I feel:

Mornings with the Master

Lord, I thank you for:

Please forgive me for:

Father, please bless:

Lord, you promised me:

I need to talk to you about:

Today's declaration:

Make time for ME:

Goals & Expectations:

Reflect & Release

66

Just when the caterpillar thought her life was over, she began to fly.

Date _____

Inner battery _____ %

Celebrate yourself - Wins for the day:

Today's struggles:

Face your feelings:

Shift your mind:

Speak to it:

MENTAL HEALTH CHECK | On a scale of 1-10, how are you feeling?

| 1 | 2 | 3 | 4 | 5 | 6 | 7 | 8 | 9 | 10 |

Describe your day in 1 word:

Dear God,

Rise & Shine

Date _____

God has never birthed a failure, now go be GREAT today.

Inner battery _____ %

Today, I feel:

Mornings with the Master

Lord, I thank you for:

Please forgive me for:

Father, please bless:

Lord, you promised me:

I need to talk to you about:

Today's declaration:

Make time for ME:

Goals & Expectations:

Reflect & Release

66

Just when the caterpillar thought her life was over, she began to fly.

Date _____

Inner battery _____ %

Celebrate yourself - Wins for the day:

Today's struggles:

Face your feelings:

Shift your mind:

Speak to it:

MENTAL HEALTH CHECK | On a scale of 1-10, how are you feeling?

| 1 | 2 | 3 | 4 | 5 | 6 | 7 | 8 | 9 | 10 |

Describe your day in 1 word:

Dear God,

Rise & Shine

"

God has never birthed a failure, now go be GREAT today.

Date _____

Inner battery _____ %

Today, I feel:

Mornings with the Master

Lord, I thank you for:

Please forgive me for:

Father, please bless:

Lord, you promised me:

I need to talk to you about:

Today's declaration:

Make time for ME:

Goals & Expectations:

Reflect & Release

Date _____

Inner battery _____ %

Celebrate yourself - Wins for the day:

Today's struggles:

Face your feelings:

Shift your mind:

Speak to it:

MENTAL HEALTH CHECK | On a scale of 1-10, how are you feeling?

| 1 | 2 | 3 | 4 | 5 | 6 | 7 | 8 | 9 | 10 |

Describe your day in 1 word:

Dear God,

Rise & Shine

Date _____

Inner battery _____ %

Today, I feel:

Mornings with the Master

Lord, I thank you for:

Please forgive me for:

Father, please bless:

Lord, you promised me:

I need to talk to you about:

Today's declaration:

Make time for ME:

Goals & Expectations:

Reflect & Release

66

Just when the caterpillar thought her life was over, she began to fly.

Date _____

Inner battery _____ %

Celebrate yourself - Wins for the day:

Today's struggles:

Face your feelings:

Shift your mind:

Speak to it:

MENTAL HEALTH CHECK | On a scale of 1-10, how are you feeling?

| 1 | 2 | 3 | 4 | 5 | 6 | 7 | 8 | 9 | 10 |

Describe your day in 1 word:

Dear God,

Rise & Shine

God has never birthed a failure, now go be GREAT today.

Date _____

Inner battery _____ %

Today, I feel:

Mornings with the Master

Lord, I thank you for:

Please forgive me for:

Father, please bless:

Lord, you promised me:

I need to talk to you about:

Today's declaration:

Make time for ME:

Goals & Expectations:

Reflect & Release

"
Just when the caterpillar thought her life was over, she began to fly.

Date _____

Inner battery _____ %

Celebrate yourself - Wins for the day:

Today's struggles:

Face your feelings:

Shift your mind:

Speak to it:

MENTAL HEALTH CHECK | On a scale of 1-10, how are you feeling?

1	2	3	4	5	6	7	8	9	10

Describe your day in 1 word:

Dear God,

Rise & Shine

66
God has never birthed a failure, now go be GREAT today.

Date _____

Inner battery _____ %

Today, I feel:

Mornings with the Master

Lord, I thank you for:

Please forgive me for:

Father, please bless:

Lord, you promised me:

I need to talk to you about:

Today's declaration:

Make time for ME:

Goals & Expectations:

Reflect & Release

66

Just when the caterpillar thought her life was over, she began to fly.

Date _____

Inner battery _____ %

Celebrate yourself - Wins for the day:

Today's struggles:

Face your feelings:

Shift your mind:

Speak to it:

MENTAL HEALTH CHECK | On a scale of 1-10, how are you feeling?

1	2	3	4	5	6	7	8	9	10

Describe your day in 1 word:

Dear God,

Rise & Shine

66

God has never birthed a failure, now go be GREAT today.

Date _____

Inner battery _____ %

Today, I feel:

Mornings with the Master

Lord, I thank you for:

Please forgive me for:

Father, please bless:

Lord, you promised me:

I need to talk to you about:

Today's declaration:

Make time for ME:

Goals & Expectations:

Reflect & Release

"

Just when the caterpillar thought her life was over, she began to fly.

Date _____

Inner battery _____ %

Celebrate yourself - Wins for the day:

Today's struggles:

Face your feelings:

Shift your mind:

Speak to it:

MENTAL HEALTH CHECK | On a scale of 1-10, how are you feeling?

1	2	3	4	5	6	7	8	9	10

Describe your day in 1 word:

Dear God,

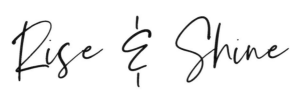

Rise & Shine

" God has never birthed a failure, now go be GREAT today.

Today, I feel:

Mornings with the Master

Lord, I thank you for:

Please forgive me for:

Father, please bless:

Lord, you promised me:

I need to talk to you about:

Today's declaration:

Make time for ME:

Goals & Expectations:

Reflect & Release

"
Just when the caterpillar thought her life was over, she began to fly.

Date _____

Inner battery _____ %

Celebrate yourself - Wins for the day:

Today's struggles:

Face your feelings:

Shift your mind:

Speak to it:

MENTAL HEALTH CHECK | On a scale of 1-10, how are you feeling?

| 1 | 2 | 3 | 4 | 5 | 6 | 7 | 8 | 9 | 10 |

Describe your day in 1 word:

Dear God,

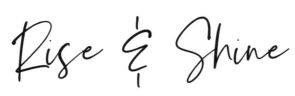

Rise & Shine

Date _____

Inner battery _____ %

Today, I feel:

Mornings with the Master

Lord, I thank you for:

Please forgive me for:

Father, please bless:

Lord, you promised me:

I need to talk to you about:

Today's declaration:

Make time for ME:

Goals & Expectations:

Reflect & Release

"
Just when the caterpillar thought her life was over, she began to fly.

Date _____

Inner battery _____ %

Celebrate yourself - Wins for the day:

Today's struggles:

Face your feelings:

Shift your mind:

Speak to it:

MENTAL HEALTH CHECK | On a scale of 1-10, how are you feeling?

| 1 | 2 | 3 | 4 | 5 | 6 | 7 | 8 | 9 | 10 |

Describe your day in 1 word:

Dear God,

Rise & Shine

Date _____

Inner battery _____ %

Today, I feel:

Mornings with the Master

Lord, I thank you for:

Please forgive me for:

Father, please bless:

Lord, you promised me:

I need to talk to you about:

Today's declaration:

Make time for ME:

Goals & Expectations:

Reflect & Release

"
Just when the caterpillar thought her life was over, she began to fly.

Date _____

Inner battery _____ %

Celebrate yourself - Wins for the day:

Today's struggles:

Face your feelings:

Shift your mind:

Speak to it:

MENTAL HEALTH CHECK | On a scale of 1-10, how are you feeling?

| 1 | 2 | 3 | 4 | 5 | 6 | 7 | 8 | 9 | 10 |

Describe your day in 1 word:

Dear God,

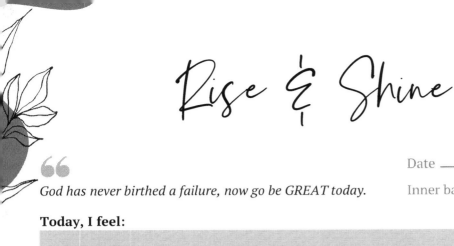

Rise & Shine

Date _____

> *God has never birthed a failure, now go be GREAT today.*

Inner battery _____ %

Today, I feel:

Mornings with the Master

Lord, I thank you for:

Please forgive me for:

Father, please bless:

Lord, you promised me:

I need to talk to you about:

Today's declaration:

Make time for ME:

Goals & Expectations:

Reflect & Release

Just when the caterpillar thought her life was over, she began to fly.

Date _____

Inner battery _____ %

Celebrate yourself - Wins for the day:

Today's struggles:

Face your feelings:

Shift your mind:

Speak to it:

MENTAL HEALTH CHECK | On a scale of 1-10, how are you feeling?

| 1 | 2 | 3 | 4 | 5 | 6 | 7 | 8 | 9 | 10 |

Describe your day in 1 word:

Dear God,

Rise & Shine

Date _____

Inner battery _____ %

Today, I feel:

Mornings with the Master

Lord, I thank you for:

Please forgive me for:

Father, please bless:

Lord, you promised me:

I need to talk to you about:

Today's declaration:

Make time for ME:

Goals & Expectations:

Reflect & Release

"
Just when the caterpillar thought her life was over, she began to fly.

Date _____

Inner battery _____ %

Celebrate yourself - Wins for the day:

Today's struggles:

Face your feelings:

Shift your mind:

Speak to it:

MENTAL HEALTH CHECK | On a scale of 1-10, how are you feeling?

| 1 | 2 | 3 | 4 | 5 | 6 | 7 | 8 | 9 | 10 |

Describe your day in 1 word:

Dear God,

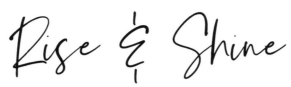

Rise & Shine

God has never birthed a failure, now go be GREAT today.

Today, I feel:

Mornings with the Master

Lord, I thank you for:

Please forgive me for:

Father, please bless:

Lord, you promised me:

I need to talk to you about:

Today's declaration:

Make time for ME:

Goals & Expectations:

Reflect & Release

> Just when the caterpillar thought her life was over, she began to fly.

Date _____

Inner battery _____ %

Celebrate yourself - Wins for the day:

Today's struggles:

Face your feelings:

Shift your mind:

Speak to it:

MENTAL HEALTH CHECK | On a scale of 1-10, how are you feeling?

| 1 | 2 | 3 | 4 | 5 | 6 | 7 | 8 | 9 | 10 |

Describe your day in 1 word:

Dear God,

Rise & Shine

Date _____

Inner battery _____ %

Today, I feel:

Mornings with the Master

Lord, I thank you for:

Please forgive me for:

Father, please bless:

Lord, you promised me:

I need to talk to you about:

Today's declaration:

Make time for ME:

Goals & Expectations:

Reflect & Release

> Just when the caterpillar thought her life was over, she began to fly.

Date _____

Inner battery _____ %

Celebrate yourself - Wins for the day:

Today's struggles:

Face your feelings:

Shift your mind:

Speak to it:

MENTAL HEALTH CHECK | On a scale of 1-10, how are you feeling?

| 1 | 2 | 3 | 4 | 5 | 6 | 7 | 8 | 9 | 10 |

Describe your day in 1 word:

Dear God,

Rise & Shine

Date _____

Inner battery _____ %

God has never birthed a failure, now go be GREAT today.

Today, I feel:

Mornings with the Master

Lord, I thank you for:

Please forgive me for:

Father, please bless:

Lord, you promised me:

I need to talk to you about:

Today's declaration:

Make time for ME:

Goals & Expectations:

Reflect & Release

" "

Just when the caterpillar thought her life was over, she began to fly.

Date _____

Inner battery _____ %

Celebrate yourself - Wins for the day:

Today's struggles:

Face your feelings:

Shift your mind:

Speak to it:

MENTAL HEALTH CHECK | On a scale of 1-10, how are you feeling?

| 1 | 2 | 3 | 4 | 5 | 6 | 7 | 8 | 9 | 10 |

Describe your day in 1 word:

Dear God,

Rise & Shine

66

God has never birthed a failure, now go be GREAT today.

Inner battery _____ %

Today, I feel:

Mornings with the Master

Lord, I thank you for:

Please forgive me for:

Father, please bless:

Lord, you promised me:

I need to talk to you about:

Today's declaration:

Make time for ME:

Goals & Expectations:

Reflect & Release

Just when the caterpillar thought her life was over, she began to fly.

Date _____

Inner battery _____ %

Celebrate yourself - Wins for the day:

Today's struggles:

Face your feelings:

Shift your mind:

Speak to it:

MENTAL HEALTH CHECK | On a scale of 1-10, how are you feeling?

| 1 | 2 | 3 | 4 | 5 | 6 | 7 | 8 | 9 | 10 |

Describe your day in 1 word:

Dear God,

Rise & Shine

❝

God has never birthed a failure, now go be GREAT today.

Date _____

Inner battery _____ %

Today, I feel:

Mornings with the Master

Lord, I thank you for:

Please forgive me for:

Father, please bless:

Lord, you promised me:

I need to talk to you about:

Today's declaration:

Make time for ME:

Goals & Expectations:

Reflect & Release

66

Just when the caterpillar thought her life was over, she began to fly.

Date _____

Inner battery _____ %

Celebrate yourself - Wins for the day:

Today's struggles:

Face your feelings:

Shift your mind:

Speak to it:

MENTAL HEALTH CHECK | On a scale of 1-10, how are you feeling?

| 1 | 2 | 3 | 4 | 5 | 6 | 7 | 8 | 9 | 10 |

Describe your day in 1 word:

Dear God,

Rise & Shine

Date _____

Inner battery _____ %

Today, I feel:

Mornings with the Master

Lord, I thank you for:

Please forgive me for:

Father, please bless:

Lord, you promised me:

I need to talk to you about:

Today's declaration:

Make time for ME:

Goals & Expectations:

Reflect & Release

"
Just when the caterpillar thought her life was over, she began to fly.

Date _____

Inner battery _____ %

Celebrate yourself - Wins for the day:

Today's struggles:

Face your feelings:

Shift your mind:

Speak to it:

MENTAL HEALTH CHECK | On a scale of 1-10, how are you feeling?

| 1 | 2 | 3 | 4 | 5 | 6 | 7 | 8 | 9 | 10 |

Describe your day in 1 word:

Dear God,

It ran in your family
until it ran into you.
God says,
``You've been
anointed
to break the cycle."

Generational curses
end with you.

It's okay to change your mind.

It's okay to have questions.

It's okay to want better.

It's okay to need help.

It's okay to say "No".

It's okay to grow.

It's okay to cry.

It's okay, Sis.

It's okay.

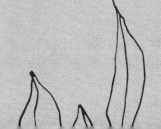

Rise & Shine

> 66
> *God has never birthed a failure, now go be GREAT today.*

Today, I feel:

Mornings with the Master

Lord, I thank you for:

Please forgive me for:

Father, please bless:

Lord, you promised me:

I need to talk to you about:

Today's declaration:

Make time for ME:

Goals & Expectations:

Reflect & Release

"
Just when the caterpillar thought her life was over, she began to fly.

Date _____

Inner battery _____ %

Celebrate yourself - Wins for the day:

Today's struggles:

Face your feelings:

Shift your mind:

Speak to it:

MENTAL HEALTH CHECK | On a scale of 1-10, how are you feeling?

| 1 | 2 | 3 | 4 | 5 | 6 | 7 | 8 | 9 | 10 |

Describe your day in 1 word:

Dear God,

Rise & Shine

Date _____

Inner battery _____ %

Today, I feel:

Mornings with the Master

Lord, I thank you for:

Please forgive me for:

Father, please bless:

Lord, you promised me:

I need to talk to you about:

Today's declaration:

Make time for ME:

Goals & Expectations:

Reflect & Release

66

Just when the caterpillar thought her life was over, she began to fly.

Date _____

Inner battery _____ %

Celebrate yourself - Wins for the day:

Today's struggles:

Face your feelings:

Shift your mind:

Speak to it:

MENTAL HEALTH CHECK | On a scale of 1-10, how are you feeling?

| 1 | 2 | 3 | 4 | 5 | 6 | 7 | 8 | 9 | 10 |

Describe your day in 1 word:

Dear God,

Rise & Shine

God has never birthed a failure, now go be GREAT today.

Inner battery _____ %

Today, I feel:

Mornings with the Master

Lord, I thank you for:

Please forgive me for:

Father, please bless:

Lord, you promised me:

I need to talk to you about:

Today's declaration:

Make time for ME:

Goals & Expectations:

Reflect & Release

66

Just when the caterpillar thought her life was over, she began to fly.

Date _____

Inner battery _____ %

Celebrate yourself - Wins for the day:

Today's struggles:

Face your feelings:

Shift your mind:

Speak to it:

MENTAL HEALTH CHECK | On a scale of 1-10, how are you feeling?

| 1 | 2 | 3 | 4 | 5 | 6 | 7 | 8 | 9 | 10 |

Describe your day in 1 word:

Dear God,

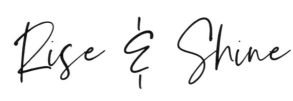

Rise & Shine

66

God has never birthed a failure, now go be GREAT today.

Inner battery _____ %

Today, I feel:

Mornings with the Master

Lord, I thank you for:

Please forgive me for:

Father, please bless:

Lord, you promised me:

I need to talk to you about:

Today's declaration:

Make time for ME:

Goals & Expectations:

Reflect & Release

" "
Just when the caterpillar thought her life was over, she began to fly.

Date _____

Inner battery _____ %

Celebrate yourself - Wins for the day:

Today's struggles:

Face your feelings:

Shift your mind:

Speak to it:

MENTAL HEALTH CHECK | On a scale of 1-10, how are you feeling?

| 1 | 2 | 3 | 4 | 5 | 6 | 7 | 8 | 9 | 10 |

Describe your day in 1 word:

Dear God,

Rise & Shine

Date _____

Inner battery _____ %

Today, I feel:

Mornings with the Master

Lord, I thank you for:

Please forgive me for:

Father, please bless:

Lord, you promised me:

I need to talk to you about:

Today's declaration:

Make time for ME:

Goals & Expectations:

Reflect & Release

"

Just when the caterpillar thought her life was over, she began to fly.

Date _____

Inner battery _____ %

Celebrate yourself - Wins for the day:

Today's struggles:

Face your feelings:

Shift your mind:

Speak to it:

MENTAL HEALTH CHECK | On a scale of 1-10, how are you feeling?

| 1 | 2 | 3 | 4 | 5 | 6 | 7 | 8 | 9 | 10 |

Describe your day in 1 word:

Dear God,

Rise & Shine

Date _____

Inner battery _____ %

> *God has never birthed a failure, now go be GREAT today.*

Today, I feel:

Mornings with the Master

Lord, I thank you for:

Please forgive me for:

Father, please bless:

Lord, you promised me:

I need to talk to you about:

Today's declaration:

Make time for ME:

Goals & Expectations:

Reflect & Release

> Just when the caterpillar thought her life was over, she began to fly.

Date _____

Inner battery _____ %

Celebrate yourself - Wins for the day:

Today's struggles:

Face your feelings:

Shift your mind:

Speak to it:

MENTAL HEALTH CHECK | On a scale of 1-10, how are you feeling?

| 1 | 2 | 3 | 4 | 5 | 6 | 7 | 8 | 9 | 10 |

Describe your day in 1 word:

Dear God,

Rise & Shine

66
God has never birthed a failure, now go be GREAT today.

Inner battery _____ %

Today, I feel:

Mornings with the Master

Lord, I thank you for:

Please forgive me for:

Father, please bless:

Lord, you promised me:

I need to talk to you about:

Today's declaration:

Make time for ME:

Goals & Expectations:

Reflect & Release

"

Just when the caterpillar thought her life was over, she began to fly.

Date _____

Inner battery _____ %

Celebrate yourself - Wins for the day:

Today's struggles:

Face your feelings:

Shift your mind:

Speak to it:

MENTAL HEALTH CHECK | On a scale of 1-10, how are you feeling?

| 1 | 2 | 3 | 4 | 5 | 6 | 7 | 8 | 9 | 10 |

Describe your day in 1 word:

Dear God,

Rise & Shine

66

God has never birthed a failure, now go be GREAT today.

Date _____

Inner battery _____ %

Today, I feel:

Mornings with the Master

Lord, I thank you for:

Please forgive me for:

Father, please bless:

Lord, you promised me:

I need to talk to you about:

Today's declaration:

Make time for ME:

Goals & Expectations:

Reflect & Release

66

Just when the caterpillar thought her life was over, she began to fly.

Date _____

Inner battery _____ %

Celebrate yourself - Wins for the day:

Today's struggles:

Face your feelings:

Shift your mind:

Speak to it:

MENTAL HEALTH CHECK | On a scale of 1-10, how are you feeling?

| 1 | 2 | 3 | 4 | 5 | 6 | 7 | 8 | 9 | 10 |

Describe your day in 1 word:

Dear God,

Rise & Shine

Date _____

Inner battery _____ %

Today, I feel:

Mornings with the Master

Lord, I thank you for:

Please forgive me for:

Father, please bless:

Lord, you promised me:

I need to talk to you about:

Today's declaration:

Make time for ME:

Goals & Expectations:

Reflect & Release

66

Just when the caterpillar thought her life was over, she began to fly.

Date _____

Inner battery _____ %

Celebrate yourself - Wins for the day:

Today's struggles:

Face your feelings:

Shift your mind:

Speak to it:

MENTAL HEALTH CHECK | On a scale of 1-10, how are you feeling?

| 1 | 2 | 3 | 4 | 5 | 6 | 7 | 8 | 9 | 10 |

Describe your day in 1 word:

Dear God,

Rise & Shine

God has never birthed a failure, now go be GREAT today.

Inner battery _____ %

Today, I feel:

Mornings with the Master

Lord, I thank you for:

Please forgive me for:

Father, please bless:

Lord, you promised me:

I need to talk to you about:

Today's declaration:

Make time for ME:

Goals & Expectations:

Reflect & Release

"
Just when the caterpillar thought her life was over, she began to fly.

Date _____

Inner battery _____ %

Celebrate yourself - Wins for the day:

Today's struggles:

Face your feelings:

Shift your mind:

Speak to it:

MENTAL HEALTH CHECK | On a scale of 1-10, how are you feeling?

| 1 | 2 | 3 | 4 | 5 | 6 | 7 | 8 | 9 | 10 |

Describe your day in 1 word:

Dear God,

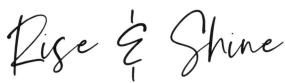

Rise & Shine

Date _____

Inner battery _____ %

Today, I feel:

Mornings with the Master

Lord, I thank you for:

Please forgive me for:

Father, please bless:

Lord, you promised me:

I need to talk to you about:

Today's declaration:

Make time for ME:

Goals & Expectations:

Reflect & Release

66

Just when the caterpillar thought her life was over, she began to fly.

Date _____

Inner battery _____ %

Celebrate yourself - Wins for the day:

Today's struggles:

Face your feelings:

Shift your mind:

Speak to it:

MENTAL HEALTH CHECK | On a scale of 1-10, how are you feeling?

| 1 | 2 | 3 | 4 | 5 | 6 | 7 | 8 | 9 | 10 |

Describe your day in 1 word:

Dear God,

Rise & Shine

"
God has never birthed a failure, now go be GREAT today.

Date _____

Inner battery _____ %

Today, I feel:

Mornings with the Master

Lord, I thank you for:

Please forgive me for:

Father, please bless:

Lord, you promised me:

I need to talk to you about:

Today's declaration:

Make time for ME:

Goals & Expectations:

Reflect & Release

Date _____

Inner battery _____ %

Celebrate yourself - Wins for the day:

Today's struggles:

Face your feelings:

Shift your mind:

Speak to it:

MENTAL HEALTH CHECK | On a scale of 1-10, how are you feeling?

| 1 | 2 | 3 | 4 | 5 | 6 | 7 | 8 | 9 | 10 |

Describe your day in 1 word:

Dear God,

Rise & Shine

Date _____

Inner battery _____ %

Today, I feel:

Mornings with the Master

Lord, I thank you for:

Please forgive me for:

Father, please bless:

Lord, you promised me:

I need to talk to you about:

Today's declaration:

Make time for ME:

Goals & Expectations:

Reflect & Release

"
Just when the caterpillar thought her life was over, she began to fly.

Date _____

Inner battery _____ %

Celebrate yourself - Wins for the day:

Today's struggles:

Face your feelings:

Shift your mind:

Speak to it:

MENTAL HEALTH CHECK | On a scale of 1-10, how are you feeling?

| 1 | 2 | 3 | 4 | 5 | 6 | 7 | 8 | 9 | 10 |

Describe your day in 1 word:

Dear God,

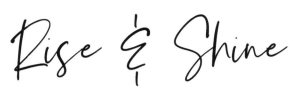

Rise & Shine

Date _____

Inner battery _____ %

Today, I feel:

Mornings with the Master

Lord, I thank you for:

Please forgive me for:

Father, please bless:

Lord, you promised me:

I need to talk to you about:

Today's declaration:

Make time for ME:

Goals & Expectations:

Reflect & Release

"

Just when the caterpillar thought her life was over, she began to fly.

Date _____

Inner battery _____ %

Celebrate yourself - Wins for the day:

Today's struggles:

Face your feelings:

Shift your mind:

Speak to it:

MENTAL HEALTH CHECK | On a scale of 1-10, how are you feeling?

| 1 | 2 | 3 | 4 | 5 | 6 | 7 | 8 | 9 | 10 |

Describe your day in 1 word:

Dear God,

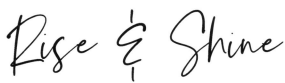

Rise & Shine

"

God has never birthed a failure, now go be GREAT today.

Inner battery _____ %

Today, I feel:

Mornings with the Master

Lord, I thank you for:

Please forgive me for:

Father, please bless:

Lord, you promised me:

I need to talk to you about:

Today's declaration:

Make time for ME:

Goals & Expectations:

Reflect & Release

> "
Just when the caterpillar thought her life was over, she began to fly.

Date _____

Inner battery _____ %

Celebrate yourself - Wins for the day:

Today's struggles:

Face your feelings:

Shift your mind:

Speak to it:

MENTAL HEALTH CHECK | On a scale of 1-10, how are you feeling?

| 1 | 2 | 3 | 4 | 5 | 6 | 7 | 8 | 9 | 10 |

Describe your day in 1 word:

Dear God,

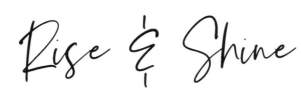

Rise & Shine

Date _____

Inner battery _____ %

Today, I feel:

Mornings with the Master

Lord, I thank you for:

Please forgive me for:

Father, please bless:

Lord, you promised me:

I need to talk to you about:

Today's declaration:

Make time for ME:

Goals & Expectations:

Reflect & Release

"
Just when the caterpillar thought her life was over, she began to fly.

Date _____

Inner battery _____ %

Celebrate yourself - Wins for the day:

Today's struggles:

Face your feelings:

Shift your mind:

Speak to it:

MENTAL HEALTH CHECK | On a scale of 1-10, how are you feeling?

| 1 | 2 | 3 | 4 | 5 | 6 | 7 | 8 | 9 | 10 |

Describe your day in 1 word:

Dear God,

Rise & Shine

Date _____

Inner battery _____ %

God has never birthed a failure, now go be GREAT today.

Today, I feel:

Mornings with the Master

Lord, I thank you for:

Please forgive me for:

Father, please bless:

Lord, you promised me:

I need to talk to you about:

Today's declaration:

Make time for ME:

Goals & Expectations:

Reflect & Release

"
Just when the caterpillar thought her life was over, she began to fly.

Date _____

Inner battery _____ %

Celebrate yourself - Wins for the day:

Today's struggles:

Face your feelings:

Shift your mind:

Speak to it:

MENTAL HEALTH CHECK | On a scale of 1-10, how are you feeling?

| 1 | 2 | 3 | 4 | 5 | 6 | 7 | 8 | 9 | 10 |

Describe your day in 1 word:

Dear God,

Rise & Shine

God has never birthed a failure, now go be GREAT today.

Date _____

Inner battery _____ %

Today, I feel:

Mornings with the Master

Lord, I thank you for:

Please forgive me for:

Father, please bless:

Lord, you promised me:

I need to talk to you about:

Today's declaration:

Make time for ME:

Goals & Expectations:

Reflect & Release

"
Just when the caterpillar thought her life was over, she began to fly.

Date _____

Inner battery _____ %

Celebrate yourself - Wins for the day:

Today's struggles:

Face your feelings:

Shift your mind:

Speak to it:

MENTAL HEALTH CHECK | On a scale of 1-10, how are you feeling?

| 1 | 2 | 3 | 4 | 5 | 6 | 7 | 8 | 9 | 10 |

Describe your day in 1 word:

Dear God,

Rise & Shine

> God has never birthed a failure, now go be GREAT today.

Date _____

Inner battery _____ %

Today, I feel:

Mornings with the Master

Lord, I thank you for:

Please forgive me for:

Father, please bless:

Lord, you promised me:

I need to talk to you about:

Today's declaration:

Make time for ME:

Goals & Expectations:

Reflect & Release

> Just when the caterpillar thought her life was over, she began to fly.

Date _____

Inner battery _____ %

Celebrate yourself - Wins for the day:

Today's struggles:

Face your feelings:

Shift your mind:

Speak to it:

MENTAL HEALTH CHECK | On a scale of 1-10, how are you feeling?

| 1 | 2 | 3 | 4 | 5 | 6 | 7 | 8 | 9 | 10 |

Describe your day in 1 word:

Dear God,

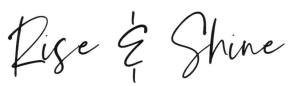

Rise & Shine

" "

God has never birthed a failure, now go be GREAT today.

Date _____

Inner battery _____ %

Today, I feel:

Mornings with the Master

Lord, I thank you for:

Please forgive me for:

Father, please bless:

Lord, you promised me:

I need to talk to you about:

Today's declaration:

Make time for ME:

Goals & Expectations:

Reflect & Release

Just when the caterpillar thought her life was over, she began to fly.

Date _____

Inner battery _____ %

Celebrate yourself - Wins for the day:

Today's struggles:

Face your feelings:

Shift your mind:

Speak to it:

MENTAL HEALTH CHECK | On a scale of 1-10, how are you feeling?

| 1 | 2 | 3 | 4 | 5 | 6 | 7 | 8 | 9 | 10 |

Describe your day in 1 word:

Dear God,

Rise & Shine

Date _____

Inner battery _____ %

Today, I feel:

Mornings with the Master

Lord, I thank you for:

Please forgive me for:

Father, please bless:

Lord, you promised me:

I need to talk to you about:

Today's declaration:

Make time for ME:

Goals & Expectations:

Reflect & Release

Just when the caterpillar thought her life was over, she began to fly.

Date _____

Inner battery _____ %

Celebrate yourself - Wins for the day:

Today's struggles:

Face your feelings:

Shift your mind:

Speak to it:

MENTAL HEALTH CHECK | On a scale of 1-10, how are you feeling?

| 1 | 2 | 3 | 4 | 5 | 6 | 7 | 8 | 9 | 10 |

Describe your day in 1 word:

Dear God,

Rise & Shine

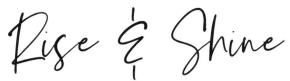

66

God has never birthed a failure, now go be GREAT today.

Date _____

Inner battery _____ %

Today, I feel:

Mornings with the Master

Lord, I thank you for:

Please forgive me for:

Father, please bless:

Lord, you promised me:

I need to talk to you about:

Today's declaration:

Make time for ME:

Goals & Expectations:

Reflect & Release

Just when the caterpillar thought her life was over, she began to fly.

Date _____

Inner battery _____ %

Celebrate yourself - Wins for the day:

Today's struggles:

Face your feelings:

Shift your mind:

Speak to it:

MENTAL HEALTH CHECK | On a scale of 1-10, how are you feeling?

| 1 | 2 | 3 | 4 | 5 | 6 | 7 | 8 | 9 | 10 |

Describe your day in 1 word:

Dear God,

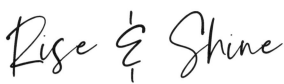

Rise & Shine

Date _____

> God has never birthed a failure, now go be GREAT today.

Inner battery _____ %

Today, I feel:

Mornings with the Master

Lord, I thank you for:

Please forgive me for:

Father, please bless:

Lord, you promised me:

I need to talk to you about:

Today's declaration:

Make time for ME:

Goals & Expectations:

Reflect & Release

66

Just when the caterpillar thought her life was over, she began to fly.

Date _____

Inner battery _____ %

Celebrate yourself - Wins for the day:

Today's struggles:

Face your feelings:

Shift your mind:

Speak to it:

MENTAL HEALTH CHECK | On a scale of 1-10, how are you feeling?

| 1 | 2 | 3 | 4 | 5 | 6 | 7 | 8 | 9 | 10 |

Describe your day in 1 word:

Dear God,

Rise & Shine

Date _____

Inner battery _____ %

Today, I feel:

Mornings with the Master

Lord, I thank you for:

Please forgive me for:

Father, please bless:

Lord, you promised me:

I need to talk to you about:

Today's declaration:

Make time for ME:

Goals & Expectations:

Reflect & Release

Date _____

Inner battery _____ %

Celebrate yourself - Wins for the day:

Today's struggles:

Face your feelings:

Shift your mind:

Speak to it:

MENTAL HEALTH CHECK | On a scale of 1-10, how are you feeling?

| 1 | 2 | 3 | 4 | 5 | 6 | 7 | 8 | 9 | 10 |

Describe your day in 1 word:

Dear God,

Rise & Shine

66

God has never birthed a failure, now go be GREAT today.

Inner battery _____ %

Today, I feel:

Mornings with the Master

Lord, I thank you for:

Please forgive me for:

Father, please bless:

Lord, you promised me:

I need to talk to you about:

Today's declaration:

Make time for ME:

Goals & Expectations:

Reflect & Release

Date _____

Inner battery _____ %

Celebrate yourself - Wins for the day:

Today's struggles:

Face your feelings:

Shift your mind:

Speak to it:

MENTAL HEALTH CHECK | On a scale of 1-10, how are you feeling?

| 1 | 2 | 3 | 4 | 5 | 6 | 7 | 8 | 9 | 10 |

Describe your day in 1 word:

Dear God,

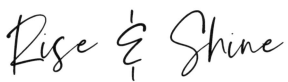

Rise & Shine

" God has never birthed a failure, now go be GREAT today.

Today, I feel:

Mornings with the Master

Lord, I thank you for:

Please forgive me for:

Father, please bless:

Lord, you promised me:

I need to talk to you about:

Today's declaration:

Make time for ME:

Goals & Expectations:

Reflect & Release

Just when the caterpillar thought her life was over, she began to fly.

Date _____

Inner battery _____ %

Celebrate yourself - Wins for the day:

Today's struggles:

Face your feelings:

Shift your mind:

Speak to it:

MENTAL HEALTH CHECK | On a scale of 1-10, how are you feeling?

| 1 | 2 | 3 | 4 | 5 | 6 | 7 | 8 | 9 | 10 |

Describe your day in 1 word:

Dear God,

Rise & Shine

"

God has never birthed a failure, now go be GREAT today.

Date _____

Inner battery _____ %

Today, I feel:

Mornings with the Master

Lord, I thank you for:

Please forgive me for:

Father, please bless:

Lord, you promised me:

I need to talk to you about:

Today's declaration:

Make time for ME:

Goals & Expectations:

Reflect & Release

"
Just when the caterpillar thought her life was over, she began to fly.

Date _____

Inner battery _____ %

Celebrate yourself - Wins for the day:

Today's struggles:

Face your feelings:

Shift your mind:

Speak to it:

MENTAL HEALTH CHECK | On a scale of 1-10, how are you feeling?

| 1 | 2 | 3 | 4 | 5 | 6 | 7 | 8 | 9 | 10 |

Describe your day in 1 word:

Dear God,

Rise & Shine

Date _____

Inner battery _____ %

Today, I feel:

Mornings with the Master

Lord, I thank you for:

Please forgive me for:

Father, please bless:

Lord, you promised me:

I need to talk to you about:

Today's declaration:

Make time for ME:

Goals & Expectations:

Reflect & Release

"
Just when the caterpillar thought her life was over, she began to fly.

Date _____

Inner battery _____ %

Celebrate yourself - Wins for the day:

Today's struggles:

Face your feelings:

Shift your mind:

Speak to it:

MENTAL HEALTH CHECK | On a scale of 1-10, how are you feeling?

1	2	3	4	5	6	7	8	9	10

Describe your day in 1 word:

Dear God,

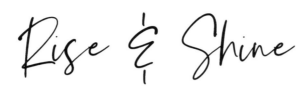

Rise & Shine

> *God has never birthed a failure, now go be GREAT today.*

Today, I feel:

Mornings with the Master

Lord, I thank you for:

Please forgive me for:

Father, please bless:

Lord, you promised me:

I need to talk to you about:

Today's declaration:

Make time for ME:

Goals & Expectations:

Reflect & Release

"

Just when the caterpillar thought her life was over, she began to fly.

Date _____

Inner battery _____ %

Celebrate yourself - Wins for the day:

Today's struggles:

Face your feelings:

Shift your mind:

Speak to it:

MENTAL HEALTH CHECK | On a scale of 1-10, how are you feeling?

| 1 | 2 | 3 | 4 | 5 | 6 | 7 | 8 | 9 | 10 |

Describe your day in 1 word:

Dear God,

Rise & Shine

God has never birthed a failure, now go be GREAT today.

Date _____

Inner battery _____ %

Today, I feel:

Mornings with the Master

Lord, I thank you for:

Please forgive me for:

Father, please bless:

Lord, you promised me:

I need to talk to you about:

Today's declaration:

Make time for ME:

Goals & Expectations:

Reflect & Release

Just when the caterpillar thought her life was over, she began to fly.

Date _____

Inner battery _____ %

Celebrate yourself - Wins for the day:

Today's struggles:

Face your feelings:

Shift your mind:

Speak to it:

MENTAL HEALTH CHECK | On a scale of 1-10, how are you feeling?

| 1 | 2 | 3 | 4 | 5 | 6 | 7 | 8 | 9 | 10 |

Describe your day in 1 word:

Dear God,

Mental Notes

Mental Notes

Mental Notes

....

....

....

....

....

....

....

....

....

....

....

....

....

....

....

....

....

....

....

....

Mental Notes

Mental Notes

Made in the USA
Columbia, SC
15 September 2021

45522897R00117